MW00614696

Reflections from a Quiet Voice

EDNA M. VANN

Copyright © 2020 Edna M. Vann

All rights reserved. No part of this publication may be reproduced, distributed, or transmitted in form or by any means without prior written permission of the author.

ISBN: 978-1-7323796-2-6

ACKNOWLEDGMENTS

I first give all thanks to God for giving me the gift of taking my thoughts, feelings, observations, emotions, prayers, fears, triumphs, and reflections to put into words that will inspire, encourage, or at least make you think. I am so blessed by the words God gives me to connect with others as they travel through this journey called Life.

To my family – I thank my mother, Beatrice C. Vann, for always encouraging me to not only scribble my thoughts on paper but to publish my work for others to read. I thank my siblings for their continued love, prayers, and support.
Thank you, Crystal, my oldest niece, for the great photos you took during our Christmas (2019) family vacation at Carolina Beach. We had no idea that one of your many photos would be used for the cover of my first book. Look at God working in your life.

I would like to acknowledge my church family at Abundant Hope Christian Church for encouraging me to write and for allowing me opportunities to share my writings with them on many occasions.

Thanks to my special friends who have read my work over the years and encouraged me to continue my quest to publish.

A special thank you to Karen Burnette, my friend and sister of Swing Phi Swing Social Fellowship Inc. for the great photo of myself that was taken during Swing Phi Swing Social Fellowship, Inc. 50th Anniversary.

I would also like to thank Monique Tuset and To Say or not Tuset Publishing, for her time, patience, and willingness to work with me and for surrounding me with the right people. Thanks to Capricia Davis for editing this book for me.

TO GOD BE THE GLORY!

DEDICATION

I dedicate this book to my mother, Beatrice C. Vann for always loving me, encouraging me and praying for me. You have asked me several times over the last two years when was I going to finish this book. It is finished! I hope that you enjoy it and that I have made you proud.

Reflections from a Quiet Voice

CONTENTS

INTRODUCTION

This book is in honor of my deceased father, William Vann who died in May of 1981. His death forced me to pencil my feelings in order to manage my emotional pain. I continued to use this tool as a means to respond to experiences and situations, to encourage myself, and to inspire others throughout my journey called life.

Reflections from A Quiet Voice encompasses a few of my personal poems, reflections, observations, considerations, celebrations, mediations and views over a period of thirty plus years. It's hard to believe I have been journaling for that long. Monique Tuset, my publisher, reminded me that I didn't have to try and fit it all in this book, which led me to believe that God is giving me provision for a second book.

Why a Quiet Voice? For those that know me I think you can attest that a "quiet voice" (peaceful, reserved, still, close) is indicative of my character and spirit. This is a trait that I must have inherited from my mother. I do my best thinking in the early hours of the morning when my body is still and my mind is calm and clear to listen to God's voice. I remember asking Brother Willie Ingram, the oldest male disciple at my church, who was also quiet and humble, a question about being a good leader because of my quiet demeanor. His response was "being quiet does not mean being silent." Brother Ingram passed in December 2019 but those words will remain with me forever.

Each writing reflects my thoughts that have been inspired from my relationship with God and it is my hope that as you read them, you will be able to connect and be inspired.

THE CHURCH

And I tell you that you are Peter, and on this rock I will build my church, and the gates of Hades will not overcome it.

~Matthew 16:18, New International Version

A Church

If I were an artist, I would paint a picture with a golden frame,
A picture of a community gathered in Jesus' name.
The people would all look different, but their souls would be the same.
For they would gather frequently, seeking salvation, not fame.

The people in this picture would comfort each other, understanding each other's pain.
Never would they tear down, talk about, or destroy each other's names.
They would meet seeking a word to help them live holy each day.
No matter who they were, what they looked like or experienced, they'd never be turned away.

This place would be led by a man with God's word.
You'd know by his teaching and the life he modeled, not by something you heard.
His life wouldn't be much different from his flock that seemed lost.
His purpose for his people would be guided by the cross.

This pastor would minister to his members and the community as a whole.
His concern wouldn't be increasing membership but saving every woman and man's soul.
The spirit of God would radiate throughout this place –
Through song, praise, love, preaching, and shouts of God's mercy and grace.

The people would be diligent in learning and understanding the word of God.
The hearts of the people in this painting would be real – no camouflage.
I kept looking at the people in this painting to see who noticed me;
Then I realized – they were there for a healing, which was far beyond what my eyes could see.

This painting was full of so much warmth, God's spirit, hope, and love.
I knew this feeling had to come from the Father above.

As I put on the last touch of paint and stepped back to observe my work,
I knew from the structure and the feeling in my heart,
I had painted a church…

ABUNDANT HOPE CHRISTIAN CHURCH

The Tree of Hope

This is not just an ordinary tree. This tree shall be our Tree of Hope guided by God's light.

The soil that this tree is planted in is righteous soil.

The roots of this tree shall represent the pastor and the ministerial staff as they feed God's WORD to God's people to become laymen and servants for God.

The trunk, which is the body of Jesus Christ, is the main structure of this tree. As long as we continue to study, believe, and follow his word, this trunk will hold the tree in place.

The branches are an extension of the trunk and shall represent the different ministries of Abundant Hope Christian Church (AHCC) such as: Men and Women's ministries, Community Outreach, Christian Education, Culinary, Music, and Usher's ministries to name a few.

These strong branches will stand the test of any storms, winds, or turmoil that comes our way as we continue to stand by his word. As stated in John 15:2, "Every branch in me that does not bear fruit He takes away; and every branch that bears fruit He prunes, that it may bear more fruit" (New King James Version).

New leaves represent new membership as the old leaves represent those that have come before us to pave the way. They will be nurtured and fertilized by the body of the church through the Holy Spirit.

The bark on this tree will be the armor that will protect us from external threats of harm.

The land and community that surrounds this tree will be blessed by the deeds of the people from Abundant Hope Christian Church.

Many years from now the people will gather at the church, holding hands surrounding this Tree of Hope;

Thanking and praising God, singing songs of Zion as we look back and remember when this Tree of Hope was planted.

The House that Christ Built

A house of worship, a church, the physical mortar where we gather weekly,
To display and demonstrate our gratitude through praise and worship.
A structure for God's people to gather to be taught
God's word and promises.

A sacred structure to aid those seeking refuge,
To mend broken hearts, eternal life is offered.
Repenting for forgiveness, judging not, but looking for unconditional love.

A building assigned a righteous leader,
To lead God's people to the promised land.
A leader who's accepted the calling and recognizes –
He must go like Moses and move like Abraham.

A dwelling of teachings and testimonies,
Of why we stayed fixed on God.
With the faith of a mustard seed,
His word is what we believe.

This house is built in our hearts;
Therefore, acts of nature, negative words, nor neglect will separate us.

The house that Christ built resides in my heart.

CELEBRATION OF FAMILY

In every conceivable manner, the family is a link to our past, bridge to our future.
— Alex Haley

You are My HERO

Mom, remember the times of yesterday and the paths
we've all struggled through?
I want you to know that we wouldn't be here today
Spreading our love, sharing our talents
If it were not for God and YOU.

I remember growing up, wearing Sharon and Joan's clothes.
A few times wearing their shoes even though they hurt my toes.
I can even reflect back to daddy using Vaseline to shine our Sunday shoes;
We always knew one of us girls would have to pray during Children's Hour,
just not sure who he'd choose.

The years of bringing in wood and drawing water from the well –
I never thought all these experiences, plus your love
Would provide me with the pride, dignity, responsibility,
And drive to succeed and excel.

The love, strength, and togetherness you've given our family can never be
replaced;
That's because YOU have been BLESSED with God's own grace.

Mom, you have always pushed us, encouraged us
Demanded that we fulfill our dreams.
Although we're stretched across the country and have different professions
You've embedded in us that a FAMILY must stay a team.

You have provided us with strength, faith, and everlasting love
From whence you have obtained your BACKBONE from the Lord above.
I can never remember a time when you doubted that we would succeed
In us you have always believed.

You are a good listener, giving good advice and knowing the right things to
say
As we bother you with our numerous problems at any time of night or day.
You never try to pass judgment, regardless of what our situation may be;
Instead you usually remind us you were once young and say, *It could've also
happened to me.*

Through turmoil, family crisis, sorrow, and encounters of distress,
YOU have kept our family together through all kinds of emotional strains, and tests.

You are our FOUNDATION, and because of that, the love we share we'll never let go.
You are more than a mother –
You've been a father, a sister, brother, friend, but most of all you are our HERO.

So whatever life offers us, whatever obstacles it may bring,
Whenever we achieve anything in life
It's because you are and have always been the
"WIND BENEATH OUR WINGS".

We Celebrate You

We celebrate your amazing strength,
As a woman and mother,
Your endurance to not only raise your children,
But to be a mother figure to so many others.

We celebrate the things that you taught us –
Independence, love, respect,
Hard work, the value of family,
Prayer and how to stand still and listen to God.

We celebrate your faith in Jesus Christ –
The prayer warrior for those in need.
He is your rock,
Which keeps our family foundation together.

We celebrate your life and the happiness you share
Through your family and friends,
What you do for others,
The countless blessings and testimonies from your soul within.

To God, for you we pray,
As we celebrate,
YOU on your 80th birthday.

Happy Birthday Mom!

Searching

I heard your message, visualized your pain.
My eyes started wailing, pouring like rain.
There's guilt on my mind, emptiness in my heart,
From a baby boy to a young man, so many years apart.

I was not in your life – don't even know your birthday, never tried to call.
I'm ashamed to say that I'm your family; no excuse for my lack of love and care.
I have no words and nothing to say, no idea how to repair.

Time can't be regained;
It will always be the past.
My prayer, my hope, is that the pain you expressed,
And are experiencing right now, will not last.

I can't expect you to contact me,
Or believe that I care.
Fifteen years since I've seen your face;
Expecting a response wouldn't be fair.

How I wish I could bring our families together, not apart.
This would be our beginning – a brand new start.

Thank You Mom

You have been my *Teacher*
I've trusted you with my life
I've learned from your *Humbleness*
Your honesty and sacrifice.

With your ability to *Accept* others
Spreading your abundance of love
Thanks for *Nurturing* me
As you prayed to God above.

Teaching me to *Kneel* for prayer
To speak with God alone
You always gave more of *Yourself*
Taking every *Opportunity* to give us a balanced home.

I've always admired your *Understanding*
That in hard times we must still walk in faith
Mom, you are a *Magnificent* woman
Showered by God's mercy and grace.

Thanks for being *Open-minded*
To thoughts of ole school and new
I dare not think what *My life*
Would be without God and you

HAPPY MOTHER'S DAY!

He is a Man... a Father

e is strong physically, but his mind and spirit
e his greatest strengths.
e controls his household with a foundation
iilt on Jesus' love and righteousness.

s success is measured
* the quality of his service to mankind –
ot by his salary, the size of his car
r when women think of him as "fine."

e stands tall in times of challenge and controversy
ealizing that it all comes from God's grace and mercy.

e cares for his children
eaching them love and respect
e emphasizes to his son that a woman's name
her God-given name, even when he's upset.

e finds time for his family
s well as for his boys
their company he's not afraid
) speak of the goodness of the Lord.

e comes to church and he brings his family – never is he alone
e acknowledges the importance of worship and prayer in his home.

e is a Man... a FATHER:

aithful to God and his family
nointed, affectionate, ambitious
hankful and trusting God's plan
umble and heaven-bound, regardless of the sacrifice
xample to young boys and men alike
ighteous and respectful is how he lives his life

e is a Man... a FATHER.

appy Father's Day!

We Honor You

We Honor You For...
Being a follower of God and placing his commandments in your heart.
Standing firm in your faith, being courageous, strong mentally and spiritually.
Being fearless of man's actions, but fearful of the God that shows you compassion.
For your forgiving spirit against those who wronged you.
Being the father that your family can depend on.
Flexible enough to spend quality time with your family, work, and church

We Honor You For...
Being the authority over your family, affirming your love daily through your words and actions.
For being awesome in the eyes of your children and,
Attentive to the needs of others and appreciative of what God provides for you.

We Honor You For...
Training your children by the instructions of God.
Teaching them how to believe and achieve their goals, turning their dreams into realities.
Being thoughtful, kind, and truthful.
Showing tough love in order to teach respect, responsibility, and honor.
The trials and testimonies you endure and are not ashamed to share.
Trusting in God, allowing him to be the source of all your needs.

We Honor You For...
Your hard work and willingness to sacrifice your comforts
For the needs of your family,
Setting high expectations for your children
Honesty about who you were, mistakes you made and
The humbleness to know that God loves you in spite of.
Being a helper to those in need, always trying to make this world a better place.

We Honor You For...
The enthusiasm of your joyful spirit, which makes us proud to know and love you.
Endurance to run the race and never give up on yourself, your children, or your family. Your perseverance to wait and see what God has for you.
The examples of your demonstration of the values you want your children to possess.

We Honor You For...
Being responsible to your family, respectful to women young and old,
Resourceful with what God has given you.
A role model to influence not only your children but all those you
encountered,
And for being in relationship with God, who is your **FATHER**.

We love you and will forever honor the men of God's House for your
Faithfulness, **A**ttentiveness, **T**houghtfulness, **H**onesty, **E**ndurance and
Righteousness

Happy Father's Day!

Family Reunion (1990)

Have you ever laughed so hard until tears just filled your eyes?
Well, if you haven't, then you should vacation at my mother's house on the 4th
of July.
We are a large and somewhat delightful crew –
Not much different from your family and you.

In order to understand the scenario to my story,
You must appreciate life, have a sense of humor, and know my family's just
ordinary.

This is a usual two-day summer event.
By the end of this family reunion, we're always wondering where all the time
went.

The festivities begin on Saturday at the crack of dawn.
Mama's up early while the dew still shines on the lawn.
She's rattling pots and pans while the smell of bacon and sausage roams down
the hall.
She's trying to be slick – that's just her usual wake-up call.

One by one, we stumble to the table.
Grumbling, *Good morning. What time did you get in?* and *Pass the coffee and newspaper.*
After breakfast, mom shouts out the agenda for the day.
For this event to be a success, *I want things done my...oh...I mean, THIS way:*

I want the house thoroughly cleaned including the windows and rugs;
I haven't had time all week, so that also includes the bathtubs.
The trash needs to be dumped, grass cut, wood chopped for the fire, and sodas put on ice.
When all this is done, we'll get dressed and prepare for your relatives – and you better be nice.

It's a cultural affair – my family is like a rack of spice.
We love each other, get along fine, and really enjoy life.
I will now take a moment and introduce the Vann clan.
When I am finished, I guarantee you to be a fan.

There's Horace from D.C. – he's the oldest of the bunch.
He's hard of hearing and never sits down to eat with us; he just likes to munch.
He usually brings his lady friend of many years;
They'll probably never be united as one because marriage is his greatest fear.

Oliver is another brother that also lives in DC

school teacher, spitting image of my dad, and never arrives before three.

ob is just arriving with Denise, Leisha, and Anjel.
hey're all wearing new clothes – brand names, so we know they are doing well.
arvin is running around, sweating because the heat is truly sizzling.
e's talking about his 10-year graduation plan, but no one is really listening.

l the way from Colorado comes Levi and Jo.
aveling across the country, he's disguising himself as tennis pro.
hey have three kids, two girls and a boy –
ich a small family; they need to have more.

y sister Joan and her family could not attend.
he probably had to work, while JJ and the boys lay around at home watching TV in
e den.

aron is complaining and asking who invited all these folks.
he next thing I know, she is walking down the road, and all I see is her blowing
noke, Jack is shortest and toughest – you will like her a lot.
he's the baby of the family, and she's a cop.

cannot forget Bill and his new bride Denise.
hey have a teenage daughter –Maketa – so I've gained another niece.
ll's personality is basically always the same;
e takes life as it is and never uses his real name (William).

ook across the field – I hear the voice of my cousin's daughter, Jenny.
here is a person standing beside her that could be Rita, Patricia, or Spinny.

unt Mildred arrives late, to be noticed and seen.
he always brings her bright personality and a bowl of baked beans.

lot of relatives and friends we always enjoy –
ur great aunts, uncles, and cousins, and there's still so many more.

he reunion is successful and on Sunday we all depart.
'e join together and pray, keeping the love for each other in our hearts.
'll probably be a whole year before we gather together at home,
ut we stay connected by writing and calling on the phone.

Williams and Vann Reunion (2007)

We gather today to celebrate love and life.
Look around – gaze at the people you see,
But don't stare too long,
Because the people you're looking at are your family.

The people in this room represent generations of great relatives,
That have come and gone –
Memories that will forever stay with us,
For we are never alone.

Family is such a special group –
And trust me, ours is no different than most.
Regardless of how much we differ, argue, and fight,
We continue to remain really close.

Different looks, interests, sizes, skin colors, hair styles, values, and beliefs –
None of this really matters when you are a true family.

Williams-Vann family, continue to love, support, and pray for each other as we
cherish this life,
And never forget – we are here only because of GOD's grace and sacrifice.

FRIENDSHIP

A friend loves at all times,
and a brother is born for a time of adversity.

~ Proverbs 17:17, New International Version

I Smiled

I Smileed...
Driving in my car remembering how we met,
I smiled and thanked God for you and us.

Friend...
Someone that knows the mess in your trunk (life),
And will help you clean it up (support you),
And carry it away (never remind you of it again).

Forgiveness...
Accepting and releasing my pain so that I can be free to accept your apology

Not necessarily forgetting but choosing not to remind me of it again.

Peace...
When a relationship ends, and you can smile again

Knowing that whatever turmoil you may be going through, God will be by your side.

Alone...
Sitting at home, waiting for a ring from my phone,
Hoping for a special person to come to visit my home.
But I spend Valentine's alone for most of the day;
No explanation to comfort my soul as to why my Valentine's Day had to end this way.

My Pride

God gave me the gift to express my thoughts, feelings, and actions,
to inspire others with my words.

When we separated as friends,
I allowed my pride, plus time, to divide and harden my heart,
I should have considered the friendship that gave us or start,
Instead I just accepted that it was over and we were through.
I refused to allow my gift to express my true feelings to you.

When illness overcame you, and I took the chance to say,
I love you, and you repeated the same.
How could I have waited so long to tell you that? I felt so ashamed.

I allowed pride and time to erase my words of hurt and pain.
You are gone now, and I will never get that chance again.

SWING PHI SWING

You...SWING PHI SWING SOCIAL FELLOWSHIP, INC.
Unique.
A wonderful addition to society,
For there is no one else like you.

Swing Phi Swing is important.
Believe it. Know it.
Swing Phi Swing allows for its realization to radiate among all women,
For there is no one else like Swing Phi Swing.

Swing Phi Swing reflects upon your feelings, experiences, and challenges,
Your hopes and dreams,
For Swing Phi Swing has much to contribute.

Swing Phi Swing will unite with you,
Grow with your differences,
Swing Phi Swing is proud...happy and like yourself
Swing Phi Swing becomes a new experience for other people.
They can learn from you,
For there is no one else like Swing Phi Swing.

The world needs Swing Phi Swing.
We can't hold back because when we do,
The world is that much less,
For there is no one else quite like you...SWING PHI SWING SOCIAL
FELLOWSHIP, INC.

OLA my sisters!

I Chose SWING PHI SWING

I always wanted to be part of a group
Couldn't figure out which one to join
I knew I had what it took
Just needed to be determined and strong.
I started to go Greek and take the easy way out
But took a glance at the white and black and quickly changed my route.

So now I'm telling everybody
That I am a SWING
I share in the growth of sisterhood
Of love and dignity

So, I chose SWING PHI SWING, and I'm proud that I did
It will always be a part of me
Yes, I love SWING PHI SWING, and I shout it out loud
My torch burns eternally.

Although membership once declined
Some gave up, some became slack
But with love and loyalty
We put SWING back on the professional track.
We refused to let the torch burn out
You see – dedication, perseverance, and determination is what we're all about.

That's why I'm telling everybody
I'm glad to be a SWING
The essence of her existence means everything to me
Yes, I love SWING, and I sing it religiously.

If you want to stagnate, stop working, or leave
That's totally up to you
I wouldn't recommend it, don't even understand it
But I want you to know that SWING will continue to grow
Forever and ever and ever…

That's why I'm telling everybody
I'm proud to be a SWING
It's the only sisterhood for me.
OLA Sisters!

Sum of a Friendly Attraction

As time passes on,
We are coming to know each other a little better.
Hopefully, as we travel with time, our acquaintance will become a stronger bond,
And we will become better "FRIENDS."

Realizing that our "FRIENDSHIP" is unique and special,
In a way that we are friends and accompany each other accordingly,
But at the same time avoiding the strength of our attractions.

Special in the sense of admiration and respect —
Admiring who we are and what we are striving to become,
Admiring each other's sense of humor, interest, hobbies, and independence,
Yet holding back and not allowing "ATTRACTION" to jeopardize the value of "FRIENDSHIP."

Respecting oneself and the ability to acknowledge friendship to maintain relationships, I wish not to know many as you.
For friends with such qualities are few.

I expect nothing more... for your character gives me laughter, thought, conversation, companionship, understanding, and
often radiant joy, as many "FRIENDS" should.

I know not where life may lead, but I do hope that wherever I will share my character and sincere personality...
Hoping we always remain best of "FRIENDS."

By Chance

What is this I'm thinking through?
Not sure of what to do.
Is it not by chance that this attraction is so strong?
Is it not by chance that my yearning to be near you is wrong?

It's not by chance that I'll take a chance to know you better.
Read my mind and my eyes –
My want for you cannot be disguised.

If not by chance, then I feel we've met before
If the situation ever arises, I'd like to be the first to meet your smile at the door.
Is all this just by CHANCE?

DEARLY DEPARTED

"That which we once enjoyed and deeply loved we can never lose, for all that we love deeply becomes part of us."
Hellen Keller

I Feel Alone

There is no preparation for the physical death –
To lose the body of someone you have known and loved all your life-long years,
To no longer touch their face, hug their body, comb their hair or wipe away their tears.

No more face-to-face conversations, laughter, crying together.
No more family vacations, trips to the store, walks in the park.
No more texting or waiting for you to come home way past dark.

What do I now do without you?
How do I go on?
How can this house remain a home?

How do I go on without you when I feel so *alone?*

In Memory of My Father, William Vann
(May 16, 1981)

It seemed like only yesternight,
That we stayed up late and watched the game.
Yes, I remember very well –
The Boston Celtics won, and their title was reclaimed.

Then the day finally arrived, and I was to graduate.
Everyone was home, ready to attend,
But for some reason the bus you rode from work was late.

It came as a shock from the telephone line;
An accident had occurred...
The call came from a familiar voice, And that's when we received the word:
A God-sent angel came through the day, and took my dear father away.

Now in memory of my wonderful dad, about four months from this day,
My heart was sadly broken, the way you passed away.
But when I saw your silent sleep, free from hurt and pain,
I could not be so selfish as to wish you back again.

Although I can't hear your voice or see your smiling face,
The lovely memory of my dear father could never be replaced.
If I could make a lifetime wish, one dream I know would come true,
I'd pray to God with all my heart for yesterday and you.

All the times I needed you and so many nights I've cried,
If my love could have saved your life, you never would have died.
I miss you sadly and long since you went.
I think of you always and try to be brave and content.

You planted the seed for our family with care.
Sometimes we didn't understand because life seemed so unfair.
Our memory of you will never part.
Although God has you in his keeping, we have you in our hearts.

I truly believe someday by the will of God, we will unite,
And everything will again be alright
As long as life and memory last
I shall remember you the way you were before you passed.

~ Sadly missed by your daughter and family

God Called

Early in life, God called you home.
Our hearts were devastated and left so alone.
We know you are traveling in Heaven far above the sky.
God, we think of Marvin as clouds in our eyes.

Your soul is at peace and your body at rest.
Although we miss you dearly, we accept that God knows best.
Oh Marvin, how we miss you, and your memories still make us cry.
Our tears represent your face like a star in the sky.

Oh God, how we miss Marvin, and we love him so much.
We thank you for comforting us with your gentle touch.

IN LOVING MEMORY OF MARVIN EARL VANN
APRIL 27, 1962 – MARCH 16, 2006

Missing You

Ten years have passed since God called you home.
It's hard to imagine that it's been that long.
Your face and actions, all the memories will never be erased.
I miss you Marvin like it was only yesterday.

I've learned from your death,
That tomorrow's not a promise, but a blessing.
Love, laughter, and living for Christ –
That was your message.

I know that you are watching over me.
There are days I feel your presence and know you are near.
I am a child of the King, I understand his plan for my life,
So, dying I will not fear
Because he paid the ultimate sacrifice.

Heaven is my eternal home;
Knowing I will see you there solidifies that.
Though I may sometimes be lonely,
Knowing we'll meet again keeps me from being alone.

I love you and miss you.
My heart will always save a place.
My being here is only because of God's goodness and grace.

Yet...I Am Unable to Cry

I am sad. I don't understand why...yet, I am unable to cry.
She encountered so much pain but was able to keep her spirit high...yet, I am unable to cry.
It is so hard watching her suffer...yet, I am unable to cry.

As we pushed her to fight for her life, knowing the odds were not fair.
Family and friends surrounded her with much love and care.
It was hard to just watch her lie there...yet, I was unable to cry.

She made peace with what God placed on her plate.
She accepted his will for her life – regardless of the journey, she knew her fate.
I believe in his holy word, his power, and have seen his works.
I can't give up. I must keep the faith...yet, I am unable to cry.

Trying to find comfort and peace to ease my sorrow and pain,
I opened her personal Bible to find the marker at Psalm 23.
Was this a coincidence that my favorite scripture was marked just for me?

I read the 23rd Psalm that always gives me comfort and peace,
Reminding me of his amazing grace that he had already released.

I walked outside her room, focused on this picture of the beach and sky.
I begged God to show me his face...as I began to cry.

I knew God was taking her to his heavenly home – a much better resting place,
I must accept his will for I know his will is never a mistake.
And yet, at that point...I was able to cry.

IN LOVING MEMORY OF ROBIN CUNNINGHAM

God Sent an Angel

It's hard to understand God's plan,
When we lose someone so near and dear to our hearts,
Especially when we've watched their pain and suffering,
From the very start.

But for a moment, think more about the life,
That this special daughter, sister, partner, and friend lived –
All the love, joy, friendship, unselfishness, laughter, and strength,
She was always willing to give.

Then hopefully during that moment,
Some of the sorrow will be eased away.
You see – God sent an angel,
To let us know she's in a good place and she's okay.

Let's cherish those special memories,
And the moments of life in time.
She would not want us weeping too much.
She told us in her own way – she was ready and would be fine.

She accepted her fate, knew her destiny, and took her last breath
As God erased all pain and suffering.
He whispered, *this is your last day, but take one more step.*
You know I've been preparing the way.

When her sibling raised the window,
An angel took her hand for her heavenly ride.
That's when her spirit transitioned,
With God to the other side.

Just hold on because God will bring comfort and healing,
In his own time, his own way.
This is when I remembered,
What Marvin Sapp would say:

He sees the tears you cry
He shares your pain inside
And sometimes you wonder why
He allows you to go through what you go through

Just know he has his hands on you[1]

There will be times when we feel all alone.
People will wonder why you're still mourning and expect you to be strong.
You may feel like this pain won't ever go away.
But at those times, just listen for the angel's voice to say:

I love you.
I miss you;
But life on earth is just a journey,
And we will meet again someday.

And when we can't hear her voice,
We still have to trust God's plan,
Because HE is God,
And HE does understand.

Weeping may endure for a night, but joy will come in the morning.

IN LOVING MEMORY OF COLETTE LASHLEY

---

[1] Sapp, Marvin. "He Has His Hands on You." Verity Gospel Music Group, a unit of Sony Music Entertainment, 2010, track 7. Genius, genius.com/Marvin-sapp-he-has-his-hands-on-you-lyrics.

It Is Well

Her life's journey is over and her earthly race comes to an end,
But isn't it sweet to know,
Her new life, with a new set of clothes, and her stylish hats,
With her heavenly father is ready to begin.

Mother Middleton lived a Christ-like life,
A devoted mother, teacher, grandmother, friend, and wife.
She will always be loved for her awesome acts of kindness,
And remembered for her unconditional sacrifices.

We know to whom her soul belongs;
God the Father, Son, and Holy Ghost has called her home.
God had long commanded her soul – therefore, death could only pierce her skin.
Because of HIS love, death did not win.

Sadness and weeping may encompass our earthly pain,
But as children of God we will see her again.
This brings comfort to our minds and souls.
Our spirits will prevail because in Jesus we know… It is Well.

IN LOVING MEMORY OF MOTHER MARGARET MIDDLETON

PRAYER AND PRAISE

Yet a time is coming and has now come when the true worshipers will worship the Father in the Spirit and in truth, for they are the kind of worshipers the Father seeks.

~ John 4:23, New International Version

A Different Kind of Love

**When you are truly in love with God,
It's just a different kind of love**

I love the seasons – so when they change, I change.
I love jellybeans but only like to eat them during Easter season.
I love football – especially the Dallas Cowboys – but will root for other teams.
I love oatmeal raisin cookies.
I love spending time with my family.
I love my mom and siblings.
I love helping people.
I love seafood but will not fry it in my house.
I love worshipping and listening to gospel music that encourages me to never give up.
I love the colors white and black.
I love making people laugh.
I love spending time and vacationing with close friends.
I love cheese.
I love playing and watching basketball.
All the things I love can change at any given time of day, month, year, or during a lifetime.

**But because Jesus is the same always,
My love for him is a different kind of love.**

In You

ank you for giving me what no other human has –
eving in me when I doubted myself,
sely supporting my needs,
ing me and providing confidence that I lost in myself.

arn for the chance to prove – not to myself, for I know my capabilities –
to share my skills and knowledge.

ι have added an entirely new outlook to my life,
ε that I've dreamed about, I cherish, love, and hope to share always.

nk you for giving me what no other human has –
ε ability to lovε. To be loved. Patience. Trust. Faith.
st importantly – A CHANCE.

Pray for the Children

Heavenly Father:

I thank you for allowing your word to prevail over our children.

Teach them to be doers of your word and not hearers only.

Help them to be thankful for what they have, to share, to do what's right, and to grow in your grace.

Keep them safe day and night. Show them how to love the world and to imitate all that is good.

Teach them not to be fearful of this world, but to recognize your power, love, and strength. Give them a sound mind in your name.

Help them to understand that they were specially made by you, that they are unique, and that you don't want them to be like anyone else.

I pray that they are obedient – that they will not conform to things of the flesh but be holy in all that they do. I pray that they will seek after your righteousness, faith, peace, and love.

Teach them to submit to their elders, to be respectful of each other, and to seek help when they are in physical or emotional pain. Help them to know that they can cast their cares on you and that you will take care of them.

Bless each adult in their lives and allow them to be living examples of you and your word. As they walk in your light, cleanse their hands, purify their hearts, and teach them to love you so that they can love themselves and others.

I most graciously give you all the honor and praise.

In your son Jesus' name, I pray for all children.

Amen.

SPIRITUAL TRUTHS

'For I know the plans I have for you,' declares the LORD, 'plans to prosper you and not to harm you, plans to give you hope and a future. Then you will call on me and come and pray to me, and I will listen to you. You will seek me and find me when you seek me with all your heart.'

~ Jeremiah 29:11-13, New International Version

Blessings

Believing in favor and knowing that your favor comes from God.

Living on the promises of God and patiently awaiting your heavenly reward.

Seeking God's advice and seeing the fruit of your labor.

Interacting and doing for others just because – no earthly reward.

Needing help and not being afraid to ask because you know your help is on the way.

Giving of yourself and receiving God's grace.

Spiritual encounters with angels sent by God.

PUSH

Push, press, persevere, practice – through whatever circumstance you may be going through.

Understand that life is hard, unfair, unjust at times, unpredictable.

See your way through by asking for strength from the Almighty, sometimes sacrificing one life in order to save another.

Humble yourself to the cause, to God, to your pride – and know that help is on the way.

Hope

Not having what you need but believing it will be there when you need it.

Facing obstacles without fear.

Believing in opportunities that you have no skills for.

A peace that covers you when words of friends and family can't get to you.

Believing in eternal life with Christ as you experience daily turmoil on earth.

Ask

When you are confused, ask for understanding.
When your mind seems weary, ask for peace.
When your soul is saddened, ask for comfort.
When your body is weak, ask for strength.
And when you are lost, ask for JESUS.

Understanding His Will

GOD is perfect – perfect in all that HE does,
Perfect in all that he says.
Perfect are his Word and Promises, and that is why I trust him.
Even when we have to experience trials, temptations, health issues, sorrow, and death,
His Word and His Will is still his perfect plan for us.

More Like You

God help me to be more like you in my daily walk, talk, and actions.
Let my words be your words.
Let my journey be led by you.
Let my footsteps be footsteps pressed in your sand.
Let what I do always be to glorify you.

God Chooses

I once heard someone say:
God takes us when he feels we are ready,
And those not chosen,
He is giving them time to get ready.

God's Promises

His promises are a pledge that something will or will not come to pass.
His promises are certain, solid – an agreement that is not temporary but
guaranteed to last.
God's promises are for all who seek him and obey his word.

Wrath of Sin

Intentional sin is like a ball of fire churning in your soul and spirit.
It gnaws at your inner core of Christian values and beliefs.
It will not allow you to rest, for you know that you have sinned.

The pain is unbearable to the believer of Christ.
For his words radiate in your mind and spirit; you know that you have
sinned.

You ask for forgiveness to ease the gnawing pain,
But it does not always come readily, even when you cry out to God again
and again.
It does not ease the pain, for you know you have sinned.

Once you come face to face with the selfishness of your sin,
Take ownership of it, confess, and repent
God will come in his own time, forgive you, and then,
In the quiet of the night, provide a solution to rectify the sin.

New Beginning

I woke up this morning to a new day – to an opportunity to start a new beginning.

My first meal today is a new beginning – to honor the physical body God has
given me.

I have the opportunity to chat with God, repent, and thank him for this day,
because it is a *new* day – a new beginning.

When I encounter my family for the first time today, it is a new day to tell them
that I love and appreciate them and to thank them for loving me.

When I enter my job for another day with my co-workers; I have no concerns
because it is a new day.

Any challenge I face, I approach differently – not on my own but seeking guidance from God and knowing that with him, I can face anything.

I can release the hurt and shame from my past. Today is a new day – a NEW BEGINNING.

Using God's Gift

When God gives you a gift, use it whenever you can.
His gift to you is to help encourage every child, woman, and man.

Now I am hurting – I need to clear my pain.
How selfish of me to think God would give it back to me again...my gift.

I refused to use my gift to clear up confusion – to apologize for my part in what went wrong.
I didn't use the gift, God's word, or my faith to make me strong.

I needed the words to express my sins, shame, and pain,
To let you and others know how much I wanted to renew our friendship again.

When I tried writing to express how I felt, I searched every corner for words,
I knew the gift given to me was buried in my selfishness – how badly I needed to be heard.

I knew God was teaching me a valuable lesson for my situation that only I'd understand,
He had given me a gift, and using it to help others was his command.

As much as I tried, not even a title, phrase, or sentence would surface into my brain.
I prayed and promised God if he'd return my gift, I'd never refrain from using it again.

Three years later, this thought, the title, just popped into my mind.
No more writers block; I knew it came from God.
He restored my gift and he did it in *His* own time.

I was so grateful for the lesson I learned.

I am a WOMAN

I am wired to be strong mentally and physically,
But I know my real strength comes from God's spiritual power and grace.
I will forever worship and be a witness for him,
Any time, to anyone, in any fashion or place.

I am obedient – not to my man,
But submissive to the Holy Spirit and what he has planned for me.
Believing in him and having faith,
Is what has set me free.

I am a miracle; the life that I've lived,
Has been a gift of God's mercy and grace.
You too are a miracle,
If you are sitting in his house today.

I admonish and encourage other women,
To love themselves and get up when they fall.
Don't' allow anyone to set your destiny,
Because Jesus has planned it all.

With all my bumps, bruises, afflictions, and strife.
When I accepted Jesus, not only did he forgive my sins,
He made me a new creature and he gave me a new life.

I lead by example for young girls to see.
I give respect, demand respect.
Compassionate, firm, direct
Because I know they are watching me.

It is my nature to help others,
And to do all that I can.
I have been petitioned by Christ, given the commandments,
And I'm headed for the promise land.

Who am I? ...I am a WOMAN:

Witness for Jesus.
Obedient to his word.
Mother of many.
Admired by plenty.
New Creature in Christ.

TESTS OF FAITH

He refreshes my soul. He guides me along the right paths for his name's sake. Even though I walk through the darkest valley, I will fear no evil, for you are with me; your rod and your staff, they comfort me.

~Psalm 23:3-4, New International Version

Storms

No wind, no rain, no floods but a lot of loss and pain.
No lightning flashing and no thunder, but loud booms and roars.
Feeling torn apart, beat up like dead fish washed ashore.

Understanding it's just a storm you're going through,
Trying to decipher the best route to take and remain true to you,
Recognizing the calm voice that will ease all hurt and pain,
You pray, *God, help me restore my faith again.*

Listening

Sitting at home all alone, listening to the rain,
Hoping it will wash away some of this inner pain.
The brisk wind blowing all around, as I recognize a familiar sound,
His voice, encouraging me not to be discouraged or feel down.

Looking for Strength

How do I draw strength from watching them suffer in constant pain?
How do I encourage them not to give up, to fight harder, when their pain becomes my pain?
How do I convince them that their physical and emotional discomfort will subside?
How can I help them when my emotional pain is a roller coaster ride?
How can I help them...?

I can draw strength from your word that has never changed.
I can pray and show you that once I accepted you as my personal savior,
My life little by little started to change — even with the pain.

I can hold your hand, walk alongside you, and pray each and every day.
And when I start to get discouraged and feel myself losing faith,
I can go to your word, lean on your promises, and know it will be restored in your Son's name.

I Will Not Stop Trusting

No matter the sickness or pain, I will not stop trusting.
No matter how many times cancer enters my circle, I will not stop trusting.
No matter how many voices I hear to make me seem insane, I will not stop trusting.

My health declines – I will not stop trusting.
My friends stop calling – I will not stop trusting.
My family members are not speaking – I will not stop trusting.

I feel like my church is not where I belong – I will not stop praying and trusting.
Death keeps knocking – I will not stop trusting.
People are killing more than they are talking – I will not stop trusting.

Children's behaviors are out of control – I will not stop trusting.
Seems that education is no longer the tool of opportunity – I will not stop trusting.
Accepting and living for Christ is more of a fad than the way to salvation – I will not stop trusting.

Loving people for who they were created to be is almost a crime – I will not stop trusting.
Families attending church together is rarely seen – I will not stop trusting.
Love conquers all – I will not stop trusting.

Speak to Your Storm

Whatever your storm may be, speak to your storm so you can move through your storm.

Live to tell about your storm, so it is no longer a storm, but only a forecast.

To storms of joblessness, poverty, and homelessness, speak – *God is my provider and He will give me what I need.*

To the storm of cancer, speak – *God is my healer.*

To the storm of depression, speak – *I am a new creature in Christ Jesus who strengthens and encourages me; I have been transformed.*

To the storm of violence, speak – *I will love my neighbor as myself.*

To the storm of abuse, speak – *no weapon formed against me shall prosper.*

To the storm of death, speak – *earth is just my journey to my final resting place is with Christ Jesus.*

To storms of hatred and prejudice towards others, speak – *you cannot win for love conquers all.*

Cancer

Cancer may have your body, but God has your mind, spirit, and soul.
This is a tough journey for you, but you will not travel this road alone.
Allow your friends to step in and help you with this trip.
Swallowing your pride to help relieve some of the pain.
You have always been there for us, so allow us to do the same.

There will be many a bumps, during this journey,
With friends you don't have to figure it out alone,
We will be with you every step of the way,
Praying, comforting, loving you each and every day,
Even when you can't hear our voice or see our face.

Get upset, cry, question God for only a little while;
This is just a journey, not who you are or even a lifestyle.
Hold onto your faith as hard as it may sometimes be.
God is your healer; just trust and believe.

Light in Darkness

I sit in darkness, but I still see light,
The light of hope, life, and love.

I sit in darkness, but I can see,
For the darkness does not cover my hopes and dreams.

Darkness reminds me of what my life was before I met the Light of the
world.

You Don't Look Like What You Have Been Through

You greet with a pearly smile.
There's no physical sign of your trials.
Your attitude and demeanor are so positive and on point.

Your eyes show no color of the tears you've shed.
No one knows the hours you cry from your bed.

Your stature is strong, your physique firm and tight.
There are no physical marks from the abuse and daily fights.

Your clothes are matching, colorful, well-kept, and neatly pressed.
Hidden are the scars, emotional pain, and stress.

No one knows your story or the pain that encompasses you.
When people see, talk, or hug – you don't look like what you 've been through.

Always worried about your children and spouse,
Tiptoeing in front of family in your own house.

You have a secret that no one else may ever know;
You survived the emotional pain, scars, and fears because God picked you up when you were mighty low.

He held you up and refused to let you fall.
He recognized your voice the first time you called.

The daily prayers and joyful praise you give him, to others, may seem really small,
But God acknowledges your prayers and gives you strength to stand – sometimes alone – but always tall.

You can't look like what you've been through,
When his blessings, grace, and mercy have been covering you.

And for your faithfulness, he has given you life…more abundantly.

SPIRITUAL
TRANSFORMATION

Therefore, if anyone is in Christ, the new creation has come: The old has gone, the new is here!

~2 Corinthians 5:17, New International Version

Make Me Over

I walked into a sanctuary, dressed to the tee.
As I moved towards the front, I felt eyes watching me.
My stylish suit, matching pumps, and right touch of makeup painted on my face,
I walked liked a phenomenal woman – slow, confident, with such grace.

I heard some whispers; I gazed at some stares,
Women wondering who I was, deacons rushing to get my chair.
What they saw was so different from what I felt or who I was –
Lonely, unsure of my future, desperate for love.

As I listened to the sermon, "MAKEOVER," was he just talking to me?
Did he know who I was – through all I was wearing, what could he possibly see?
I started to feel uncomfortable, and a part of me wanted to leave.
My legs felt too weak to stand; I was wobbling at the knees.

This minister started speaking about what we do to hide our pain,
The money we spend on clothes, shoes, make-up, and jewelry is insane.
He looked like he was speaking just to me, and I felt so ashamed.
You see, I was the phenomenal woman, and I knew how to play the game.

The clothes to hide my loneliness, promiscuous behavior, the other life that I lived,
The events of my past that I knew God could never forgive.

The makeup to cover the bumps and bruises.
Everything that was going on in my life was total confusion.

My pumps made me stand upright, to make me strut with grace,
But I was stumbling and falling 'cause,
I'd let go of God's hand and could no longer see his face.

This man of God announced that earthly makeovers lasted for short periods of time.
He started telling us about another makeover that was righteous and so divine.
I started to feel strength in my legs as I sat up straight.
My mother had always told me that giving my heart to God was never too late.

He then said something about how good and merciful God can be,
I looked myself over, thought about my circumstances, and started to
believe, *Even for a wretch like me.*
I always thought God was looking for perfection,
And all he wanted me to do was take a step in the right direction.

This preacher mentioned that God wouldn't ask questions,
And he would cover even my past.
This transformation would not be like the makeup or clothes I was wearing;
God would make me over, and for an eternity it would last.

He gave me permission to celebrate, dance, and shout God's name.
He said God would remove my old friends, bad habits, and release my
shame.
My new spiritual makeover would give me a second chance, a new life, and
a different kind of fame.

He reminded me that it wouldn't be easy;
There'd be haters at every corner and every place.
And at that point I felt God's arms around me;
He whispered in my ear, *"Just walk in my footsteps, and I'll always plead your
case."*

Just A Man

I once was just a man, like any other man,
Focusing on my physical physique to impress women,
Saying and doing what I wanted to,
Why? Because I can...just being a man.

Living in this gifted earthly space, obtaining as many worldly goods as I can,
Not recognizing it doesn't belong to me,
Living as...just a man.

Head of my house, trying to do it all on my own,
Moving fast but standing still, leaving me feeling all alone,
Pride won't let me ask for help...being just a man.

Desperate for answers, tired of doing the same things, nowhere to turn,
Needing someone stronger than me to show me a different plan,
Can't sleep at night, body restless, don't know who's wrestling with my spirit,
All during the day, such dismay...just like any typical man.

All I knew was there had to be a better way,
And then I met the *real* Man,
Who gave me a second chance when I repented of my sins,
Accepted and followed his word and believed *I CAN*.

I would no longer be just a man,
But a *godly* man, willing to embrace his plan,
To preach his gospel as best I can.

LIFE LESSONS

Life can only be understood backwards; but it must be lived forwards.

~Søren Kierkegaard

OLDER AMERICANS

Optimistic about what lies ahead.
Leaders in the church and community.
Dainty, yet demanding and devoted to the cause.
Enthusiastic. Experts on life.
Respectable and respected. Religious. Realistic about the future.

Ambitious. Accepting.
Mature-minded.
Efficient. Eager to learn new things.
Rigid, and at other times, radical.
Imaginative. Independent.
Cautious. Courageous. Calm. Confident.
Articulate. At times, arrogant.
Neat. Noisy.
Sarcastic. Sensitive. Stubborn. Sense of humor – we've got it. Successful in life because we are *serious* about life.

Thoughts that Make You Go...

Attack the issue, not the individual.

Love someone who hurt you – Jesus did.

Don't get angry with people you don't care about. It requires too much energy.

Have perfect love for an imperfect people.

Meet people where they are, and meet them at the level on which they can receive it. You may have to love them at that level.

When you hold on to history, you do so at the expense of your destiny.

If you can't save the relationship, save yourself.

It is possible to love those you cannot manage?

When you reach a mountain, do you want God to take you *over* or *through* the mountain?

Do you want God to show up in your circumstance or take your circumstance away?

Life Is

Life is about choices.
Life is about experiences.
Life is about making mistakes.
Life is about working hard for what you want.
Life is about pain and joy.
Life is about accomplishments.
Life is about loving others even when you don't feel liked.
Life is about giving of yourself and not waiting for a receipt.
Life is about standing still.
Life is about sacrifices.
Life is about living and dying.
Life is about learning.
Life is about being led by the Holy Spirit.
A good life is being in relationship with the Holy Spirit.

Why Wait

We often have visions of what we want to do later in life.

As we get older – why wait?

Why wait for our muscles to age, our movement to slow down, before running a marathon?

Why wait for the things that bring you joy, as you go about your day looking for happiness?

Why wait for that special person to have children before you recognize you already have family?

Why work, work, work before you take a vacation?

Why wait for a medical alert before scheduling an annual check-up?

Why wait for someone to be kind to you before showing kindness?

Why wait to find love with someone else when God already loves you, and *you* love you?

Why wait...?

Dreams

I know not what the eyes of tomorrow may bring.
I can only hope that in hindsight, it will find us sharing,
Seeing past the ole' visions of yesterday,
And bringing adventures for today.
Sight appears only as we see it.

Looking only for pleasant dreams and thoughts,
Knowing not when or where they may take us,
For at any time, blindness may occur,
And lose sight of all that ever was,
But holding fast to memorable dreams.

Time...You Can't Get It Back

I wish I had the courage to tell you how you made me feel.
Pride took over, and it was too late.
Time allows you to do anything you want if you act on it,
But it won't let you wait for tomorrow or go back and undo your mistakes.

Time does not erase yesterday's pain and sorrow,
But it will give you space to believe in tomorrow.

Words vs Actions

Your actions are more hurtful than your words.
Your words I can defend or choose not to hear.
Your words I can dismiss and choose not to address.
Your words can be forgiven,
But your actions are a visual image that remains with me – can't be erased
or removed.
When I see the image, I feel the pain of a dart.
Your words can be forgiven, but your actions stay with my heart.

Aging Out Loud

When I was a little girl, I used to think getting old was something that would never happen to me. As I became an adult, I used to think that when I got a little older, I wouldn't do certain things. And now, as I celebrate being an older American, this is what I want the younger generation to know...

Yes, we still remember the days of our youth – and yours too. We are not forgetful or losing our minds; we just have too much to remember.

We may have lost some of our hearing, but we are not deaf. We hear the loud noise you call music. For some reason you think you must yell when you speak to us, but you don't – if you speak to our good ear.

Our knees may sometimes become weak. If you see us walking slowly, just grab our hands and walk with us – just as we held your hand as a child when you were learning to walk.

When you hear us repeat ourselves, you don't have to remind us that we've said that before. Instead, indulge us – we indulged you when you constantly repeated our name...*momma, momma, momma!*

Take the time to talk with us, listen to our life experiences, and try to learn something from them. As a child, teen, and young adult we repeatedly listened to your stories about what happened at school, your first date, when you got your heart broken, and about how hard life is.

Don't look at us strange because you think our clothes don't match. Who said that plaids and stripes don't go together? Who promoted you to the fashion police? Don't forget – we were the ones that taught you how to dress, shine your shoes, and wash and iron your clothes.

When you see us resting our eyes in church, we are not always asleep. We may be taking a moment to rest them from the long nights of staying up with you when you were sick or worrying if you would make it home safely. Our closed eyes could be us praying and silently praising God.

Be patient with us on the highway. Don't honk your horn if we sway over into the other lane or because you think we are driving too slowly. We were the ones who took you out on the road before you even had a permit and taught you how to drive so that you could pass the driving test.

Don't complain about the many junk drawers in our kitchen. It was those drawers that provided you with school supplies, band-aids, thumbtacks, tape, pencils, pens, and tools to fix whatever was broken.

Don't push past us in malls or church because you think we are walking too slow. We don't have to walk fast through life anymore. Instead, we have learned to let grace and mercy be our steppingstones. Maybe you need to slow down too – just because you are walking fast doesn't necessarily mean you are going anywhere.

Don't look at the amount of gray in our hair and try to calculate our age. Each strand of gray hair represents our life experiences. Our battles. Our challenges. Our victories. Each child that we have constantly prayed for because they didn't have enough courage or sense to pray for themselves.

Don't look at us as "aged" …we are OLDER AMERICANS.

We are Observant. Lovable. Dedicated to a cause. Enthusiastic. Reliable.

We are active, mature-minded adults. Energetic. Respected. Intelligent. Christians. Adventurous. Notable saints, believing that because of our faithful journey we will have eternal life on the other side.

So, keep living and praying that you reach our age and possess the wisdom, grace, and humility that we do – so that one day you too will be an older American.

My Definitions

BLESSED *adjective* \ *bless·ed* | \ *'ble-səd*
I went to bed last night with physical aches and pains, with mental anguish that would not allow me to rest. But...
... because I awoke this morning, I was feeling mighty BLESSED!

FASTING *intransitive verb* \ *'fastiŋ* \
1. Giving up physical desires to strengthen my spiritual relationship with God through intimate time with him
2. Decreasing my physical needs to focus on my spiritual needs for forty days

JOY *noun* \ *jȯi* \
I'm at my lowest point, but I know God will not keep me there

LOVE *verb* \ *ləv* \
Like it's a fruit for survival

LIVING *adverb* *liv·ing* | \ *'li-viŋ* \
1. Celebrating those things that most people take for granted – breathing, smelling, sweating, hearing
2. In spite of, but God

PRAYER *noun* \ *'prer* \
Praising God for what he has already done and believing he will take care of the rest

RETIREMENT *noun* \ *ri-'tī(-ə)r-mənt* \
1. To rest the physical and mental body for a short period
2. To transition from work to home without feeling alone
3. To shift your mindset of constant problem-solving to planning at your own pace
4. To complete tasks for everyone else and not get paid, just appreciated

VICTORY *noun* *vic·to·ry* | \ *'vik-t(ə-)rē* \
1. Knowing that what God has planned for my life is bigger than I can ever imagine
2. Losing a fight and realizing that from the beginning, the battle wasn't mine...it was the Lord's

THE WORLD TODAY

I doubt if there is any problem in the world today - social, political or economic - that would not find a happy solution if approached in the spirit of the sermon on the mount.

~Harry S Truman

Who's Watching Our Children?

Our children encounter so many challenges in this world from day to day
Who's reading their faces and what they dare not say?
Are we really listening to their words or just hearing a voice?
Are we accepting their actions and allowing them to make their own
choice?

Who's paying close attention to our babies
As they grow into young ladies and men?
Who's teaching them about God, heaven, hell, and sin?

How do they deal with divorce, single-parent households, verbal abuse?
Violence and bullying in school?
Who's modeling and teaching them that with God, life will not always be
easy —
But trusting in God is cool?

Do we know their friends, or are they spending most of their time at home
and alone?
How much time are we allowing them to educate themselves on the
internet
Or texting, on Instagram, in group chats — constantly on their cellphones?

Who's watching our children as they try to gain their self-worth?
Are we allowing social media to teach them about sexual activity, peer
pressure, drugs, violence, depression
And that success is measured by money and stuff?

Do we know what type of education our children receive every day?
Who's visiting classrooms, conferencing with teachers, helping with
homework?
Or showing up at school because that's just what parents do
But if you've never stepped foot in their school, then you wouldn't have a
clue.

Are we allowing our children to just exist, not contributing to society at all?
Are we constantly reminding them that
Listening to obscene music, using profanity, provocative dance and dress
Will not render them any applause?

Who's teaching them work ethics, to be respectful with their actions and words
To pray daily, never quit, to look a person in the face when they are speaking
To get back up and brush their feelings off when they fall?

Who's hugging and praying with our babies before they leave home each day?
Helping them to understand once you walk out the door you may be judged and treated differently because of the features of your face
And that your prayer is for them to return home safe.

You ask who's watching the children…but I ask where are the adults that'll make that sacrifice?
To find a child and prepare them to live a God-fearing life?
Who's going to teach them about this man, called CHRIST?

Created by God

You don't have to love me.
As a matter of fact, you don't have to like my gender,
The color of my skin or eyes, the length of my hair.
You don't have to like how I dress, who I vote for, or my religious preference,
But you must and will respect me as a child of the living God,
Because what he created no man can destroy.

My Moment of Prayer

Father God,

I stretch my mind, body and soul to you for protection and understanding.
When does the violence end?

Amen.

My Reality

If I am a Black male or female, my life expectancy has been cut short,
Not by my own actions or measures, not from health issues I have acquired,
But due to hate and fear of those that choose to assume,
Because I am louder than they want me to be.
Or because I questioned their motives and intentions.

I am not submissive to their unjust physical demands.
They see my posture, my clothes, my hair and characterize my beliefs.
Those in authority who should be ready to serve and protect me...even because I am Black,
Instead they use that as an excuse and assume I am a threat.
So, they choose to eliminate their assumption...because I am Black.

I Cry

I cry for innocent children,
Being shot and killed.
I cry for the pain of parents losing their child –
How can that void be filled?

I cry for children that get up and go to bed in fear,
Not free to play outside, go to school, church, or the mall.
All these senseless acts of evil and killing.
Yes, I am appalled!

I cry because of the increase in violence that has spread throughout this
nation.
I cry for families that have to hide for fear of deportation.
I cry because I no longer recognize my country of love, respect, and liberty
for all.

I cry because our elected leaders are selfish – hungry for power, not Christ-
like,
Using their selfish energy for the wrong fight.
I cry because though I pray without ceasing and try to walk by faith, not
sight.
There are days that my soul has a hard time finding the light.

I cry because I won't accept this as my norm,
But I don't know what to do.
I want to stop my cry, Heavenly Father,
So, I pray for strength, understanding, and the will to not conform.

I stop the cries.
I dry my eyes.
Heavenly Father, I give these tears to you.

Climate Change

I can't sleep; this increase in violence is weighing heavy on my mind
I find myself on my knees PRAYING, pacing the floor, crying all the time.

Why are people so evil and full of so much hate?
When did the climate of our world change?
When did we stop loving people and lives became a Russian roulette game?
The management of our country like some political corporation with no shame.

Shootings and mass killings are about to be the norm
We need to clear more space for the dead, rather than jails for those who refuse
to conform
To the laws of our Constitution, our USA land
People killing on sheer HATE – just because they can.

Adults afraid to go to the mall, concerts or clubs, to dinner, or to worship at
church.
Children no longer view school as a safe place to learn
Instead of being excited, parents are kissing their kids off to school
And wondering if they will return…safely.

When did the climate change, that we rescue and feed animals
But place humans to live in tents and cages?
When the topic of how to permit people to get guns
Is discussed more than affordable housing and increasing minimal wages?

Where is our great country, once respected for its power and wealth?
The land of the free, liberty, and justice for all.

Where people of all nations gather
To work, educate, love, and worship their God of choice,
Not to listen to the daily ignorance of insanity of one voice?

When did our climate change to the degree that free is no longer FREE?

Christmas...Have we Forgotten the True Meaning of the Season?

Christmas has become so commercial.
The true meaning seemed to dissolve from our minds.
We are focusing less on "celebrating the birth of Christ,"
And turning our attention to things less divine.

Christmas conversations used to be solely about the birth of Christ,
Baby Jesus lying in a manger and the wise men that traveled from afar.
Now our conversations are more about us and what we want,
How much we should spend, or if I should purchase that new car.

Christmas should be about helping others,
Random acts of kindness, happiness, a season of great joy,
Not stressing over how we're going to extend our credit,
Just so we can have more.

Christmas is a rescue mission,
Remembering that Christ was born to save a dying world from sin;
Immanuel, "God with us."
From the beginning to the end.

Shepherds spreading the good news of his son's birth,
The sacrifice of God's gift to us,
Not Santa Claus in a red suit dropping gifts on Christmas Eve,
Or fancy wreaths and decorations that adorn our Christmas trees.

Christmas is about families coming together –
Love, unity, and creating memories that will be cherished,
And establishing traditions that will last forever.

We should demonstrate the meaning of Christmas daily, helping our
fellowman,
Being mindful of those less fortunate, willing to provide,
A meal, a gift, or kind words – an extension of our humble hearts and
hands.

Most of all, Christmas is about love – a Savior, born in a stable, not a
hospital,
A father (our Father) that shared his son with us for our sins,
That we might everyday share that same love with one another,
In hopes of seeing Christ again.
Merry Christmas...

What I Know about Children

Children are not born into a world knowing the difference in color,
Whether it's a crayon or someone's skin.

Children are not born with hate in their hearts,
But if they are surrounded by it, hear it in the community, they will choose it.

Children will smile at you if you smile at them.

Children will be kind to those who are kind to them.

Children will model the behaviors they learn,
Watching adults at home, school, church, or on TV.

Children will become better readers if they are read to.

Children will enjoy school and value education when we push them to perform beyond their expectations.
Assist them with homework and encourage them to talk about their day.

Children will learn to share when they are taught it's better to give than to receive.

Children will learn to pray when you pray with them.

Children will learn responsibility when given chores and praise for a job well-done.

Children will learn the true meaning of friendship,
When they observe their family being friends with each other.

Children will be respectful to adults when adults are respectful to them.

Children will love themselves when they are reminded of their beauty –
Their talents and individuality that were formed from God's own image.

Children will always strive to do their best when they are not compared to someone else.

Children will enjoy church when they attend with their parents, taught the stories of the Bible and encouraged to participate in church activities.

Children will learn to be productive adults if they are made to work and be responsible as a child.

Children will feel at ease talking to adults when adults take the time to listen to them.

Children will believe "They Can" when positive words and prayers are spoken over them each day.

Children will learn to love God when they see the God in us.

When Does the Killing Cease?

When does the killing cease?
How do we find peace?
Where do we seek justice in a majority world unlike us?
Who do you trust?

For there's no consequence,
When police officers are killing black folk.
This is not a joke.

Who is doing all the unjust killing?
Why does it seem like violence besieges just us?
When will all this injustice, this violence cease?
Where and how do we as black folk find any rest or peace?

THE END

ABOUT THE AUTHOR

Edna M. Vann graduated from North Carolina Central University in 1981 with a Bachelor Science in Recreation. She has also earned a Master of Science in Therapeutic Recreation (1985), Master of Arts in Special Education (1988), and a certification in School Administration (1991). Her 35-year career in education consist of Special Education Teacher, School Administrator at the middle and high school levels and Senior Administrator for Special Education Services. She is also trained as a facilitator and mediator. After retiring in July 2018, Edna started her own business, Parent to School, LLC, to support parents in advocating for their school-aged children and understanding the special education process. She is an active member of the Raleigh Graduate Chapter of Swing Phi Swing Social Fellowship Inc. Edna attends Abundant Hope Christian Church in Durham, NC.

Edna enjoys spending time with her family, vacationing with friends, participating in church and community activities, walking, participating in Senior games, and spending time at the beach listening to the ocean. Edna pledged Swing Phi Swing Social Fellowship, Inc at North Carolina Central University in the Spring of 1980. She is currently a member of the Raleigh Graduate Chapter of Swing Phi Swing Social Fellowship, Inc.

Do you want to be an author?

To Say or Not Tuset publishing is a company designed to empower you in writing and coach you to become an author. Offering full services from editing to graphic design, To Say or Not Tuset can be your one stop shop in making your dreams a reality.

To learn more information, please visit: https://www.moniquetuset.com/publishing

Made in the USA
Columbia, SC
23 September 2020

21313750R00052